Salon Buzz: Marketing and Management Ideas for Ultimate Success

By Dennise S. Cardona

Salon Buzz: Marketing and Management Ideas for Ultimate Success

To Hector,

Thank you for being my four-leaf clover.

Table of Contents

Foreword _____ 1

Introduction _____ 3

Salon Buzz Checklist _____ 10

Chapter One: Creating a Successful Mindset _____ 11

Chapter Two: Getting Organized _____ 23

Chapter Three: Attracting a Winning Team _____ 37

Chapter Four: Standing Out in the Crowd _____ 53

Chapter Five: Providing Exceptional Customer _____ 71

Chapter Six: Increasing Profits _____ 79

Chapter Seven: Getting Social – Online _____ 95

Chapter Eight: Maintaining Value _____ 117

Endnotes _____ 125

Foreword

My first encounter with hairdressing occurred in my aunt's basement when I was twelve-years-old. My cousin needed a haircut. We just happened to come across a pair of scissors and a comb, so I dove into her hair like I was Vidal Sassoon. I combed, sectioned, recombed, resectioned, and redid all of this for about an hour before I snipped my first piece of hair.

That first snip was all it took for me to fall in love with the art of hairdressing. After that, I dreamed of hair and of chipping away at frazzled ends until they sprung up, smooth and precise. Before long, I invested in proper tools and began offering haircuts to willing participants. In high school, I was the go-to stylist. Fellow students would line my parent's living room, waiting their turn. And, when I finally graduated high school and stepped foot in cosmetology class, I thought I would explode from the excitement. A successful career soon followed, and if it weren't for my allergies, I'd still be standing behind a chair, spending my day frolicking in heads of hair.

So, this takes me to my next love: management and marketing. I focused all my energy on these two areas in college and have made a career out of them. I've managed and marketed everything from salon services and products to higher education, and have learned a great deal about leadership, branding, promoting, writing, designing, and online marketing. In fact, I learned so much that I am bursting to share this knowledge. So, here I am. And, here is everything I've learned along the way.

Dennise Cardona

Introduction

Don't aim for success if you want it; just do what you love and believe in, and it will come naturally. - David Frost

Chances are if you're reading this book it's because you have a burning desire to be in control of your destiny. At some point, you've probably already asked yourself the fundamental question – *Why am I going into business for myself?*

We all have personal reasons that bring us to the point when we leave the safety and security of a steady paycheck job and opt instead for the adventurous thrill of business ownership. Often we're seeking freedom, flexibility, challenge, spirited competition, and other *get-out-of-the-comfort-zone factors*. The one element, however, that should be present for all seeking to make a living on their own is that they love what they do.

If you love what you do, then consider yourself a million percent ahead of those who don't. That love will drive your passion and see you through the twists and turns of business ownership.

Additionally, equally important to possessing a deep love and passion for your business is having a plan. A plan is critical. Without this roadmap, you are apt to get lost.

So, let's get started. Shall we?

# #

I once worked with a girl named Chloe who said to me, "I'm going to open up a hair salon and spa."

"But you've only been cutting hair for two years," I said to her. "Are you sure you're ready for that?"

"It's easy," she said, blowing a wisp of her bleached hair out of her face. "Anyone can do it."

"Do you have a plan?"

"A plan?" Chloe cracked up at this. "Yeah, I've got a plan, alright. I plan to plop a chair and sink into a room and call myself a business owner."

"But, you have no business experience other than working a register at the gas station and now here. How will you know how to balance the books and manage supply and demand?"

She curled up her lip. "Oh please. I don't need to know all that. Who cares if I don't know a debit from a credit? That's why I'd hire an accountant. Besides, I'm talented. I've got more clients than I can service. And, I'm also tired of giving away forty percent of my income to our greedy boss."

I always thought of our boss as generous for giving us sixty-percent. "It can't be easy running this salon," I said to her.

"Please! How hard can it be? All the boss had to do was rent a storefront, decorate it, put an open sign on the front door, and make a whole lot of cash. Who cares about that strategic planning nonsense she's always carrying on about? I'm going to wing it! I'm all about being spontaneous. With the full spirit of adventure behind me, I'll figure it out as I go along. I don't know why I didn't think of this sooner."

Thirteen months later, this eager, jump-out-of-an-airplane-without-a-parachute-girl crawled back into the salon, begging for her chair back. She blamed her landlord for screwing her over and causing her business to fail.

Going into any business venture without a plan is like gambling. You might get lucky and break out of the gate like a winning horse on race day. On the flip side, you could stumble and break your knee before you even cross the starting line.

Relying on chance is a surefire way to fail.

Everyone deserves a fair shot at success. What we do with that fair shot is up to us, and the choices we make with it can make or break our venture.

Every one of us can succeed. Climbing up to and achieving dreams, even surpassing them, is possible for anyone willing to apply focused effort on learning, understanding, and following through with the necessary actions. Take the time in the beginning to build a rock solid foundation by planning properly.

This step is imperative. It will guide every other action you take. Think of your business as a new house. When selecting a contractor, you have a choice between someone who promises to build it and have you living in it faster than you could drive cross country and back or someone who requires a full year to set everything just so. Impatient and excited to get on with the process, imagine that you opt for the contractor who promises instant gratification. You've got a life to life, after all!

So, your trusty contractor gets moving. One day you're looking at a blank sandy lot, the next day you come back, he's already poured the concrete to the foundation. Perfect!

Within two months, you're in. You've splurged on the furniture with all the savings you received choosing this wonderful contractor who 'gets it'.

Ah, your home, your palace.

Your house is the envy of all. You've got party after party planned. You wonder why anyone would over analyze and over plan building a house when yours is perfectly built in a third of the time.

Let's fast forward a few months, long after you've hosted your thirteenth dinner party and showcased your digs all over Facebook for all to see. You're standing on the street corner with your neighbor admiring your palace and wallop, a storm rushes in. You run inside to your palace thankful to be under such gorgeous shelter. You venture to the basement to grab a cold drink from the beautiful bar you've equipped your home with and you step into a couple of inches of muddy water. Soon, you've got yourself a raging river. Within two weeks, your palace sinks into the earth, and all your pretty possessions drown in a sea of grime.

You may at this point, sink into a state of hysteria, asking how this could've happened. Your friendly neighbor turns to you and reminds you that it took him a full year to build his house because they reinforced it and secured its grounding before a single brick was laid. He also chose to build on the higher, rockier ground instead of the soft sandy dune nearest the lakefront.

If only you had taken the time to conduct due diligence, maybe you would've discovered the many flaws. By taking the time to research the area, the contractor, and the pros and cons of building close to the lakeside, you could've saved yourself a boatload of financial burdens.

The same is true in business.

Most anyone can lease a storefront, fill it with furniture, slap an open for business sign on the front door along with a lively bell chime, and call themselves a business. If you really want to do it right, you would add due diligence to the front of that list. Know what you are getting into before you take a step.

One thing is apparent, by ensuring your footing is grounded, balanced, and strong, you're increasing your abilities to build something truly magical, something long-standing, and something powerful enough to sustain even the toughest blows.

So just what does separate the savvy from the not so savvy? I sat down with Allyson Myers, Managing Director of

Myers Marketing Group, LLC in Atlanta, GA, and she offered some valuable insights into this curious question.

Whether you are planning to open a salon/spa, or already did and feel completely in over your head, or could just use a bit of tweaking to get to the next level, this book is for you. We'll explore the various components that go into creating, growing, and sustaining success in the salon/spa industry.

Ready to succeed? All you need is a willing, determined, and focused mind, and you're half way down the golden road. To make it the rest of the way without stumbling, just read on...

Catapult Checklist:

- Make the love of what you do the number one reason you're going into business for yourself

- Plan for success with a business, financial and marketing plan

- Lead with a contagious spirit

- Create and stick to a budget

- Work smarter, not harder, with a system

- Attach deep emotion to your venture

- Expect more, get more

- Define your brand and what makes you unique to your target

- Measure and quantify your efforts

- Surround yourself with a winning team

- Be consistent with everything you do

- Rev up promotions with creative ideas

- Add value to your services and product offerings

- Get online and interact for increased profit potentials

- Think outside the box to add dimension and value to your offerings

- Do what it is you do best, all the time

Chapter One – Creating a Successful Mindset

I want to do it because I want to do it. - Amelia Earhart

What's the first example that comes to mind when you think of success? Is it wealth? Is it paying the monthly lease on time? Is it selling a bottle of blue fingernail polish to one of your most conservative clients? If you're Chloe, perhaps it's snapping your finger and creating a dream spa where everything just magically falls into place and where not one iota of planning is needed. What is it for you? It's important to get clear on this, so you know if you're heading in that direction.

When you open those salon doors for the first time as 'the boss', you want to do so with a flair of confidence, knowing that what you're about to create is your own little world with your name and style written all over it. The world will either embrace it or criticize it, and the choice depends mainly on your leadership style.

No one dreams of struggling. Certainly Chloe didn't. She seemed shocked that her small army of stylists wasn't producing the green stuff fast enough.

"Aren't stylists supposed to come out of cosmetology school fully-trained?" she asked me on her second day back at the salon. "I had my hands full with my own clients. How did they expect me to stop everything and teach them how to fade sideburns or foil without bleach bleed?" She rolled her eyes and continued blow-drying her locks.

"Maybe they needed more structure?"

"I didn't want to be a babysitter. Those girls should've known how to upsell a haircut into a color. It was just so frustrating."

Like Chloe, many people set out with good intentions only to find themselves hanging precariously from a cliff overlooking unchartered territory. One of the first steps in building a strong business foundation is determining its management structure. Will you be hands-on, involved, an active participant, and an informed decision maker? Your answer to these should be a very emphatic YES!

MANAGE WITH CARE

From staffing, to creating a system of tasks, to setting expectations, managing is and will always be the most important element to a successful business. Without planning this stage properly, you may as well just let go of the cliff's edge and drop now. If you're not keen on pain, then you can avoid it. Here's how: manage with care and lead with passion.

If you're a serious entrepreneur with a burning desire to be on your own, you've probably already asked yourself these critical questions: Am I cut out for managing a business? Do I have the necessary skills and traits to lead a team of people who are counting on me? Will people listen to my ideas? How can I be the best at this?

These are all valid questions that should be explored. The great news is anyone with a willingness to learn and model her actions after those who have preceded her successfully can get to a point where she can answer affirmatively.

How much you succeed as a leader depends entirely on how much you're willing to open yourself up to the risks of learning new skills and applying them in real life situations where employees, clients and external stakeholders are depending on you to take bold action. Your success will ultimately depend on your team's success as they operate under your business and your umbrella. If your umbrella is riddled with holes and bent wires, you're going to get wet.

Leading takes more than technical ability. We've all known creative geniuses who can turn shaggy heads of hair into modern marvels. But can these artists lead? In other words, as an artist, do you bring more to the table than just an exceptional gift to create jaw-dropping styles? Do you have that contagious spirit that others are eager to latch onto and follow? Is this spirit so defined that even the hair coiled around the drainpipe would unravel and follow you around your pretty salon if it were possible?

If you're scratching your head wondering, don't despair. You can hone in on the different areas of expertise that you need to possess and shine them up just like pomade on a frazzled hair shaft. What needs to happen when you increase your role from specialized technician to leader is a readjustment of focus. Modeling your behavior after someone you admire, someone who is doing exactly what you wish to be doing, is a great place to start.

Here are some key aspects on which you need to focus: think like a strategist, pump up your spirit, set realistic expectations, and crank up that confidence (You're going to need it!).

THINK LIKE A STRATEGIST

Chloe said to me, "I worked at least seventy hours a week right off the bat, yet, I still couldn't bring in enough money to cover my expenses. I still don't understand what went wrong."

"Were you cutting hair that whole time?" I asked her.

"Well, no, not the whole time. But still, I was there laboring over the business, tidying up, folding towels, answering the phone, booking appointments; you name it. Yet, somehow, it wasn't enough. I had no more of myself to give."

Like Chloe, many people spend a lot of time at their business and think because they do they deserve the money to roll in and smother them in giddy pride. A lot of people try to save money by doing all the work themselves. From a production perspective, Chloe wasted a lot of time doing activities she could have paid someone else to do instead. Had she hired someone to do such activities, she would've freed herself to take on more client. This could've generated double, triple or even quadruple what she saved in doing these tasks herself. Time management is about evaluating your worth and determining how best you can enjoy your time doing the things that will ultimately profit your business more.

A strategic thinker is one who looks at the big picture and decides where she wants to take things a year, two years, even ten years later. She sets her expectations on par with her goals so she's "working smarter" and "not harder". Many people work very hard and very long hours and are not nearly as effective as others who work less time.

The goal should be to be effective and focused in the time that you're working, so that you're not just running around the salon wasting time doing things that you really don't need to be doing and that someone else could be doing. The priority should be to focus on contributing to the growth of the business at the time that you are there. Ensure that anything you're spending your time on is worthwhile and the most effective way of doing what it is you're doing.

Say for instance, you spend thirty hours a week developing promotions, direct mail pieces and a newsletter, and then you decide to send these out to all of the people who have visited your salon. Would the return on investment of this strategy be as effective as spending five hours a week in the reception area greeting current and future loyal customers instead? Five hours of schmoozing and monitoring the work that your stylists are doing versus thirty hours in the back creating direct mailers and newsletters yields BIG differences. Which is more valuable? Working harder or working smarter?

Would you accomplish much more if you simply hire someone with a background in graphic design to create your brochures, cards, ads, etc.? Start analyzing how you spend your time, then ask yourself, "How can I be even more effective?" Your brain will search for this answer and respond with actionable steps.

PUMP UP YOUR SPIRIT

What is one of the first things you think of when you wake up in the morning or when you go to bed at night? Does it have something to do with your business venture? Do you find exciting ideas popping into your brain at all times of the day? Is there a jotter pad on your passenger seat brimming with random thoughts on how to grow your business? Is the notes application on your IPhone overflowing with creative snippets? Do you have a burning desire that is so strong you swear it could propel you up in the air if you were attached to a hot air balloon? Please say YES!

I really hope you say yes because that enthusiasm, my fellow entrepreneurs, is the gem that will carry you through and sustain you beyond any curve, disappointment, or challenge that may throw itself on the pathway to your goals and dreams. Such intense enthusiasm is necessary. That enthusiasm is the juice that will keep your motivation flowing. That enthusiasm will also help you attach a deeper meaning to your actions, one that goes beyond the superficial goal of money.

What is it about being a leader in this dynamic industry that excites you? Get down to the real, honest-to-goodness reason you are pursuing this venture. Let it tickle your soul and cause you to rise up against any adversity, any obstacle, any naysayer. Perhaps it's the idea of being in control of your own destiny? Or placing yourself in a position where you can positively affect your staff's lives? Or is it the freedom of being able to create the environment you want to live in on a consistent basis? Find your reason and let it marinate until it becomes so much a part of your driving force, nothing will be able to pry it from you.

Allyson Myers says: "Try to remember the reason you first got into this business; why you started in it. Hopefully, it wasn't just an expectation that you're going to make a ton of money by working for yourself. Hopefully it goes way beyond that to a point where it's because you just love what you do and you want to be surrounded by it all the time. Ideally, you want to do it the way you think it should be done because you are fully engaged in and passionate for all things salon and beauty. Keep that passion and drive alive, so if a time presents itself when you maybe get off course a bit, you can reattach yourself to that center of where your passion is today."

As time passes on and your business takes on a life form all its own, because it will, you may feel burnt out and have to go back and realign yourself with this centered passion. Burnout happens often and is typically the result of boredom, stress, lack of direction, or lack of anchoring to a goal. So, by going back and redefining or recognizing the passion that brought you here in the first place, you can eliminate burn out and refocus on what it is you do best.

Identifying the anchor that gives life to your dreams is critical. Perhaps it's having an element of giving back to the community, or building a team of motivated professionals, or the artistic freedom to enhance the lives of others through your own interpretation of the hair artistry. Whatever it is for you, it's the pinnacle of your purpose and spirit, and needs to be defined up front.

Exercise:

Set aside time to brainstorm. Sit in a quiet room where you will not be disturbed. Set a timer for ten minutes, and jot down everything and anything that comes to mind with your feelings on why owning a salon is so important to you. Don't censor

19

your answers. Don't edit or worry about typos and grammar. Just write freely for ten minutes, allowing all thoughts to pass through you onto the paper or screen. When the timer goes off, review your writing. I am positive that you will discover your passion and purpose weaved into it. Pull it out and rewrite it into a simple sentence or a series of bullet points that you can carry with you, hang on your wall, and use as part of your personal mission statement.

SET REALISTIC EXPECTATIONS

What is it really like when you are trying to get your salon up, running, and off the ground? Are your expectations based in reality? Let's take a look at Chloe again and see how she experienced the reality check of salon ownership.

"I had to cancel my trip to Mexico because I couldn't leave the salon for a whole week and expect to come back with it in working order." She fidgeted with her round brush, yanking hair from it with the tough teeth of her comb. "I fully expected freedom. I saw myself working three days a week and spending the other four shopping, going to the beach, and hanging with my kids. I never anticipated the massive amount of time I'd need to spend there. I mean, how is it that our boss can take every other day off?"

"It's taken her many years to get to that point," I said. "When she first started out, she was here all the time."

"I just never thought it would be so much work. I had my new lifestyle as boss all worked out in my brain, and, let me tell you, it was nothing like that."

Just as with a fresh garden, growing healthy, vibrant fruits and veggies takes time, patience, and hard work. Cultivating the soil, planting the seeds, and then watching the plants come alive and grow to their fullest potential takes time, patience, and love. It is no different when you open a business. How you look at the process will determine your enjoyment and ultimate success. Just as a gardener can never expect to plant seeds and simply watch them grow without removing weeds, watering the soil, feeding the new plants, and taming wild branches, neither can a business owner expect a salon to open one day and grow into a successful enterprise without proper nurturing.

Myers explains that within the first couple of years, it's important to understand the changes that may, most likely, occur in your current lifestyle. Long hours and the need for dedicated focus are inevitable, as you need to be available and consistent with salon hours and staff.

It's dangerous for any new salon owner to believe that she can enjoy the fruits of her labor before the fruits are planted. This can be especially dangerous if a new salon owner hires a salon manager to cover her responsibilities. Hardly anyone is ever going to be as vested in the success of the business as you. Upon first hire, this salon manager may do enough to get by, but they are probably not going to dedicate their full attention for the seventy-hour weeks that are required in a startup situation. This isn't to say that eventually, once you've created a management system through thoughtful study, analysis, and careful implementation, you can't ultimately hire someone to manage.

With proper planning, you can carve out a system over time that can be readily understood by a salon manager, and by everybody that works with you. You'll recognize at a certain point that you have the right people in place and an easy to follow system. At this point, the salon starts to run more efficiently, even when you're not around. Your presence will not be necessary at the level it was in the first few years, but you'll still need to be very involved to keep efficiency and success sustained.

Biggest takeaway is to set your expectations on par with reality so that you go into your venture focused and clear.

Chapter Two – Getting Organized

Always do your best. What you plant now, you will harvest later. - Og Mandino

CREATE A SYSTEM

Just like chili peppers and cumin are vital ingredients to a rocking chili recipe, so are rules and strategies to a thriving business. Build a model of your ideal salon, and the road to achieving this goal will be less rocky. A model will help your business work for you instead of the other way around.

You might be thinking, *what the heck is a model and how do I build one?* No need to scratch your head on this one. If you've ever worked for someone other than yourself, chances are you've seen one and probably even had to sign that you read it from cover to cover. Think of it as a guidebook that helps you stay on the road more traveled versus the off beaten dangerous paths with all their twists, turns, and surprise cliffs.

This guidebook, or operations manual, simply documents every task necessary to keep your business thriving. Its purpose is to direct anyone you hire to be able to pick up the pieces should you not physically be there. It allows a staff member to figure out exactly what needs to be done, when, and how. No one can be expected to never take a vacation, and this handy guidebook will ensure when you return from your quiet oasis, that your salon is still standing and clients are still filtering in and out as rapidly as your breath would be in a fifty yard dash.

With a guidebook, your salon can consistently operate on an efficient level. Every member of your team should be given a copy and sign that he/she has read it and understands its contents. Keep it simple, bullet-pointed, and organized so that it can serve to support your daily rules and purposes within your salon and spa.

Plug everything into this manual and redefine it as you grow and learn more. If you wish to have every patron greeted with a compliment whether it be, 'hey, I love that sweater' or 'wow, what a great smile you're wearing today' then type that in there. If you intend to reward loyal customers with a complimentary bottle of shampoo on their birthdays, then paste that in there, too. If you wish to have black aprons worn by all staff, then add that, too. You get the picture. Every last operational detail should be entered. Nothing should be left up to the whimsy guesses. [1]

Craft rules that make sense to the type of environment you're creating. Consider things from dress code, to cleaning the salon, to serving the client, to greeting the client, to booking the next appointment, to suggesting retail products, to inviting them back for another appointment.

Unsuccessful salons make up the rules as they go along, resulting in everyone being confused and no one getting it right. In the case of Chloe, had she implemented a guidebook, maybe she wouldn't have had to crawl back to her old job and beg for her chair back.

"So all I had to do to get the girls from wearing slutty low-cut tank tops," she might've asked me had she known, "was type out a sentence in a manual that told them that I wanted them to wear black crew neck tees with a pink apron?"

And to that, I would've replied, "Exactly!"

You see, people love rules whether they admit it or not. We all need them. We crave them. Otherwise we run around this world with too many opinions of what should and shouldn't be a priority, and that can lead to massive disaster and chaos.

MANAGE MONEY

How tempting would it be to take your first few months of profit and go blow it on that new dress you saw in the window at Saks' Fifth Avenue, buy that new car you've been eyeing in the dealer's lot, or book that cruise to the Caribbean? You deserve it after all, right? You've been working your butt off getting your business up and running, and you've succeeded! You've got clients rolling in, a team of stylists booked for two weeks out, and you're doing better than just breaking even now. You're profiting! Yahoo! Time to celebrate and spend that money! Right?! If you believe this, then you're in trouble.

The truth is, and this can be hard to swallow for some, a smart business owner will reinvest any profit back into the business for at least eighteen months, even if they are seeing a steady cash flow. Those willing to do this are smart because, not only are they setting themselves up to comfortably pay their bills, they are also placing themselves in a position to seize opportunities.

I'm sure it won't come across as a big surprise when I make the claim that the first eighteen months of any new business can be unpredictable. You must (A) account for any lulls and (B) increase your marketing and promotion in order to increase your business. If you're okay with maintaining a level of just good enough, then you wouldn't need to reinvest all your profits. But, if you are looking to consistently grow, you need to.

Don't take your eyes off the goals you've set. To achieve them takes focus, a certain level of frugalness, and a whole lot of budgeting and forecasting. If you put your profit dollars to work, then you'll increase your chances of achieving your revenue goals much faster. Set your revenue goals and stick to them. Look at your sales records and recognize the trends so you can determine the potential to gain even more clientele. Analyze and understand areas of low penetration within your targeted demographic or within a certain service offering and find new ways to tap into them through your profits.

You must keep a vigilant watch on your sales. Then, using your marketing tactics, appeal to the demographic where you're looking for that higher penetration. If you know there is a demand for certain services, and you just need to get word out to the right target for them to soar, then put your dollars toward those areas. If you see room for expansion to gain a higher success rate, then forgo the pretty black dress and pour those dollars into reaching that expansion.

Creating and sticking to a budget is critical. When setting your budget, keep the following typical expenses in mind:

Lease payment, loan repayment, insurance, equipment, utilities, repairs, telephone, internet, bank fees, taxes, payroll, professional fees, business and professional license fees, education, inventory, advertising, printing and designing fees, and signage.

SET GOALS

Measurable goals are critical to salons who strive to grow and impart a legacy. Ask a successful entrepreneur what she does to ensure she sets and executes actions towards achieving these goals, and she is likely to tell you that she writes them down and hangs them up where she is inspired to read them every single day.

To achieve such goals, you must take action. This often requires taking leaps, facing risks, conquering the inner voices in our heads ranting impossibilities, avoiding the sink into self-pity when things don't go as planned, and standing up to those who try to dismantle momentum with their stories of failure.

The truth is, no one is going to understand your goals the way you do. They will not understand what fires up your passion, what keeps you going day and night to chase your dreams, and what not achieving them would do to your spirit.

So it's critical you hold tight to your truths, convictions, and ideals and understand them intimately.

The world is filled with unrealized potential and unfulfilled dreams. It is also filled with amazing feats, unstoppable fervor, and limitless inspiration. You have a choice – to take action on your dreams or allow others to steer you in other directions.

The most effective way to plan for the future is to set goals. These goals should be realistic, attainable, timely, and action-oriented. Goals aid us in getting organized, and by getting organized, we're better equipped to handle the ups and downs we'll experience along the way.

In setting goals, ask yourself these questions:

- Where do you see your business in 5-10 years?
- Do you want to outgrow your space? If so, by how much?
- Will you add more services?
- Do you wish to hire additional staff?
- How will you cope with changing trends? Through education, in-house training, webinars?
- What if your target up and moves out of your neighborhood? How will you cope?

DRAFT A 'LIVING' MARKETING PLAN

A good marketing plan will keep you on track. Plan your plan, then follow your plan. Have a guiding framework at the get-go, then adjust it in monthly increments.

Keeping your finger on the pulse of your marketing plan creates a certain level of energy, flow, and life, which is exactly what you should want for the lifeline of your salon! Strategy, which in this case is simply seeing a market potential and realizing the importance of promoting to that potential, will set you apart from the competition.

ELEMENTS OF A STRATEGIC MARKTING PLAN

What really makes a strategic marketing plan come alive and tick with enough beats to stay vibrant is one that is organized, thoughtful, and most important, written down. The elements it should include are:

Your salon's target markets – male, female, families, trendsetters, hipsters, professionals, conservatives, of-the-wall types, pink hair, spiked hair, you get the picture…

Financial goals – (What level of increase and at what frequency do you want to increase your revenue? Really think this through and ask yourself the vital question: How can I make this happen? What steps can I take today, tomorrow, and next week to ensure that I achieve these goals?)

Activities – Will you invite a hair color expert to train your staff on the latest foil techniques? Will you host a wine-tasting gala in your salon to promote a new brand of nail polish? Are you going to make Wednesday's from 1 pm to 3 pm upgraded spa pedicure days for the month of October?

Action plans/strategic implementation plans – How will you achieve activities step-by-step? For events, list out the major tasks that need to be done and by what date, who's in charge of what task, and who will work the events.

Timetables – Create goals for starting and implementing all contents in your plan.

Budget – How much will each activity cost? Research and negotiate costs, then stick to your budget.

Methods for measuring results – Will you rely on web analytics to see how many people visited a registration page to sign up for an event? How many people clicked into an HTML email? How many people received a notice about a promotion and how many of them actually purchased? Make every action measurable so you can better decide where to spend your time and money. If you're not reaping the harvest in one area, you may need to plant somewhere else.

A STRATEGIC MARKETING PLAN EXAMPLE

Salon 123's Strategic Overview | *Fall 2014*

The marketing objectives for Salon 123 are to (1) build an awareness of our salon's services and products across new markets and market to prospective clients and local employers, (2) strengthen salon's online presence through a redesign of the Web site to include more multimedia video, interactivity and social media networks, (3) advance and refine event marketing through new, supplemental formats (spa parties, charitable events, and themed girl's night out packages), (4) increase revenue ten percent over the next six months.

Our plan is to continue to engage clients/prospects through a variety of cost-efficient, cost-effective marketing channels with a message that highlights the following:

- Salon 123's ranking of Best Salon and Spa in 2013
- Salon 123's contributions to local charities
- Niche services offering one-on-one consultation
- Exceptional staff and highly-trained professionals who are widely attentive to current trends

Our marketing strategy consists of the following mediums and are the responsibility of Salon 123's Marketing Coordinator and myself:

- HTML email communications

- Redesign Website (*Launch date: Summer 2015*)
- Increase website functionality – more interactivity
- Enhance website's how-to information, including links to articles and resources
- Increase website's multimedia video
- Add blog to website
- Increase cross-marketing opportunities with locals

Social Media Networking to include:

- Facebook Fan Page Goal: Get 30 new 'likes' a month
- Twitter Goal: Get 30 new 'followers' a month
- LinkedIn (icon/link)
- YouTube Salon 123 Channel Goal: To upload one new video monthly
- Blog Goal: To publish one new blog a week (will hire a blogger interested in writing about beauty and trends)

Event Marketing:

- Mother/Daughter Spring Getaway (annual)
- Cut-a-Thon to benefit local animal shelter (annual)
- Renewed Hope Massage day to benefit local breast cancer survivors (biannual)
- Local Hero Kick off (annual)
- Girl's Night Out Events (monthly). Need to evaluate logistics and resources for feasibility.

Subscriber-based Email:

- Create an online subscriber-based email list to market events, tips, product and promo specials, and other matters of interest.

We will measure the overall success of our activities through online analytic tools that offers stats on open rates, click rates, impressions, conversions, new fans, new followers, and interactivity of community. We will evaluate effectiveness of in-person events through feedback follow-ups, average revenue generated, and overall increase in client base by end of fiscal year 2015.

Overall, our marketing strategy is aimed at cultivating a larger target market, enhancing our strong online presence and providing prospects/clients with social networks, networking opportunities and resources that fulfill our promise of being the destination for beauty, expertise, and a community of friends.

# #

With such a plan in place, you will be more apt to stay focused, directed, and on target throughout the year. Plan it, write it, and review it often.

PLAN FOR THE FUTURE

The inherent goal in getting organized is to ultimately get to where you want to go. And, the best way to get to where you want to go is to take a step back and seriously consider where it is you want this rocking salon of yours to take you. Take the time to visualize this, swallow it, and let it marinate.

Again, ask yourself these questions: Where do you see your salon in five years? Ten years? Will you outgrow your space? Add more services? Or perhaps you will take on a nutritional/wellness expert? How will you cope with changing trends? What if your target up and moves out of your neighborhood? Can you cope?

These are challenging questions that need to be well thought out and answered. Nothing stays the same, and nothing should, especially in this industry where change is nurtured and favored. Once you see what's ahead of you and decide on what gets your heart pumping fastest, you can harness all that wonderful energy and focus it directly on your new successes.

Chapter Three – Attracting a Winning Team

Everyone enjoys doing the kind of work for which
he is best suited. - Napoleon Hill

We've all heard a version of this saying: you're only as great as your weakest link. So, as business owners, it would behoove us to make sure that any weak link is stronger than our competitors' shining stars.

HIRE THE BEST FOR YOUR BRAND

A successful businessperson is one who knows what is happening at any given time, with any given employee, and with any function in the salon. She is the matriarch, the one employees look to for guidance, and the one who creates the rules and follows them alongside everyone else. She is the one who offers protection, hope, and insights. And none of this can happen without full dedication and an acute knowing of just how far she wants to take her staff and her business.

In the initial planning stage, before the interviews begin, before the first staff meeting takes place, and before the door swings open on grand-opening day, you need to design your vision for these new employees who will help catapult you to higher levels.

Some questions to ask in the creation stage:

- How many stylists do I need?
- What level of experience do they possess?
- Do I want them fresh out of school so I can train them?
- Do I want a senior stylist to take the training role?
- What type of clientele will we be servicing? What kind of team would fit this clientele?
- Should I require them to have a following? Of how many clients? Should I provide walk-ins to help further their growth?
- Am I looking for a spunky or sophisticated team?

These are just a few of the questions you want to ask in the initial stages of development. It's imperative to know where you're going so you can properly plan to get there.

Whether you're opening a new salon/spa or are trying to reel in more control and structure to an existing one, one of the most critical attributes a successful businessperson can have is to consistently be aware of all that is happening around her.

You can create the prettiest salon in the world, but if it's filled with incompetent, untrained staff, you'll spend your days staring at the pretty walls instead of enjoying the bubbly action of a salon in full service mode. To get your salon to this level requires paying attention to the fine details happening around you, not just in your chair.

If a stylist is lacking skill, you need to know this before her unruly cuts turn your salon upside down. If one of your manicurists consistently leaves nails jagged, you need to know this. If one of your skin care specialists is leaving green exfoliating goop along the client's jawline, you need to catch this.

Paying careful attention and taking the proper steps to remedy the situation before it spirals out of control is a large part of being the boss. This often requires stepping out of the comfort zone. For instance, you may need to pull a stylist from the floor who may need more training, or to provide the actual training and the guidance, or to be willing and able to fire an employee if the training is not effective.

Another thing to keep in mind is that people tend to be more committed to employers who are committed to them. So, it makes sense that an employer who acts just as committed to an employee's success as to her own will be less likely to have a team of slackers.

HOW TO CREATE A WINNING TEAM

Share your Vision:

Empower your staff by communicating what their overall purpose is to the salon, to the clients, and to each other. Respect their values and beliefs and work to center their purpose around these shaping factors. Each person brings unique talents, creativity, and value to the team. Take time to recognize these attributes.

Find out what makes them tick:

Create a survey and ask about topics such as commitment, trust, communication, and conflict resolution. Get to know how they think and how they perceive the world. How committed are they to their careers? What does it take to earn their trust and respect? How do they communicate? Are they silent, bold, argumentative, or defensive when dealing with conflict? Each person is unique, and it's critical for employers to tap into this to forge a cohesive working climate.

40

Develop a proactive system:

Set ground rules for communication, conflict resolution, problem solving, and giving and receiving feedback. Perhaps it's a meeting where everyone gets five minutes to gripe. Then, you take their gripes, let them marinate, and within twenty-four hours return with a win-win solution. Don't wait until a problem escalates out of control to solve it. Be proactive.

Set Expectations:

The importance of setting expectations can't be stated enough. Be clear in job descriptions, tasks, roles, and acceptable behaviors. Occasionally, you may encounter those employees who are just plain bad communicators. They are the type of people who argue about the sky being midnight blue over periwinkle. They feel attacked when offered constructive criticism. They make you want to throw your hands up in the air and fire them right there on the spot. But, maybe they are so talented that to do so could hurt business in the short term.

Staying focused on what you want and expect will encourage dialogue to flow in a direction that empowers. Even in conversation, it is critical to keep focused on a goal. If your goal is to create an understanding, then speak from your heart, as you would want reciprocated. Avoid negative forms of distilling information, such as manipulation, argumentation, or criticism. [2]

Harness the fun with team building:

Have fun, let loose, get out of the box and mingle in the world outside the salon walls. Go bowling, golfing or dancing. Volunteer together at a children's hospital or animal shelter. Offer salon services for a day and donate all proceeds to a charity. Anything to work together in spirited fun will help break the monotony, increase vitality, and pump up the team spirit.

Train:

In this industry, styles and trends change quicker than crazy weather patterns. What people learned ten years ago has passed, and many great artists have introduced new and improved methods and products to take client's styles up a notch or two. Invest in your staff's education to keep ahead of the curve. Your bottom line would thank you if it could. Stay on top of what's the latest and greatest in the field. Always put yourself at an advantage by being on the cutting edge and staying focused on training through seminars, videos, magazines, and demonstrations.

In addition to keeping up with education within the industry, consider enhancing their skills in peripheral areas of interest such as marketing, communications, public speaking, and selling. Not only will you be forging a fantastic valued relationship with your staff, but also you'll be gifting them with empowerment to grow as individuals and professionals. Education only benefits. It never hurts. Don't be afraid of it. Embrace it. You will attract star staff members who value themselves and who value you.

Offer incentives:

Who doesn't love receiving rewards? Everywhere you look, businesses are offering valuable assets as incentives to purchase their goods and services. These big businesses aren't doing this on a whim. They have spent hundreds of thousands of dollars researching effective ways to stimulate and motivate minds. And, if it didn't work, they wouldn't be doing it still. Why reinvent the wheel on something tried and true? Take their same successes and make them yours on a staff level. Not everyone will be driven by the same factors, so this is where understanding your staff becomes important, just as important as it is to understand your customer. Get to know your team and discover what excites them. Maybe it's Kohl's Department Store, maybe it's a movie and dinner, maybe it's donating to a charity, or maybe it's flexibility in a schedule. Find out what it is and build incentives around them.

COMMUNICATE EXPECTATIONS

If you want employees to wear blue on Wednesdays, you need to tell them that you want them to wear blue on Wednesdays. If you want employees to leave their cellphones in the storage room, then you need to tell them. Be very clear on your expectations so the staff understands.

In another example with Chloe, she seemed genuinely confused with why her team of stylists left dirty towels hanging from the shampoo bowls and waxing sticks jutting out of the wax bowl.

"It was truly disgusting to walk in each morning because I never knew what I would find. They trashed the place. It never failed. I always had to wipe up globs of color off the shampoo bowl before my clients could recline backwards. And the hair! They'd leave the hair on the floor while they smoked out back. I felt like a nag, always after them to clean up."

Without a system in place outlining expectations, people who are unable to manage themselves may run around like pigs in mud. All Chloe had to do was draft a task list and charge each employee to complete their assigned ones each and every day. The importance of a clean salon should be innate, but it's not always. Sometimes it's the simplest, most obvious things that need to be communicated. If people know right from the start what is expected, they'll perform. And, if they don't, well, you're the boss.

SCHEDULE TEAM MEETINGS

Meetings are vital to keep a team moving forward together. They allow for regrouping, reassessing, understanding problems, and finding solutions. Done effectively, they can serve to build excitement and team spirit. Take these four critical steps:

Create a meeting agenda

To stay on track and on task, ask staff to forward agenda items to you ahead of time. Staff will feel empowered knowing their ideas are important to you and that they will have a chance to voice concerns and questions. Then, print and distribute the agenda during the meeting.

Keep meetings brief

Concise (under one hour) and frequent (at least once a month) staff meetings will allow for more streamlined communication among staff. This will strengthen goals, momentum, and sharing of information.

Establish ground rules

List your primary ground rules on the agenda so everyone is clear on expectations. Examples of ground rules are: participation, focus, momentum, and creating solutions to problems.

Close effectively

End on time, and always end on a positive note. When wrapping up the meeting, summarize the main agenda items, next steps, solutions, and who is responsible for taking action on open items that need attention. Then, set your next meeting.

Schedule monthly meetings and make them fun! Perhaps create a potluck lunch where everyone brings in a dish. Set ground rules to keep the peace, keep it flowing, and to stay on time and task. Create an agenda ahead of time by asking each staff member for an entry. They will feel involved and be more apt to stay alert and open. Pass out the agenda at the beginning of the meeting with timetables so people know their limits. Have a plan to get back on task should the discussion veer off on tangents. Don't allow it to become a gripe session. Allow presentations of problems, but require a well-thought out solution, as well.

BUILDING TRUST

As a salon owner, you will be challenged with communication breakdown at some point or other. It's part of the business game. You will struggle with getting employees to see your viewpoint. You might stop and think, *gosh if I could only get them to see the point, we wouldn't be having these issues.* To no avail, we can't get them to see our point!

But why? What's happening?

What's happening in situations like this is a breakdown in empathy and trust. Empathy, in its most simplistic definition, is when we can truly understand, relate to, or imagine the depth of another person's emotional state or situation. Without empathy, trust doesn't form easily. With it, great progress can be made. And, in business, isn't this our goal?

Here's how to do it.

Act with Compassion

When a person feels threatened, they snap into protection mode, building up walls too tall and thick to pass. As employers, we may be passing along our own fears and insecurities to our employees, feeding this threat without even realizing. Tune out of the fear frequency, and instead listen to their feelings and recognize them as valuable. Admit how you feel, and have the courage to be vulnerable. This will open pathways to honest communication.

Understand their Point of View

Even if we don't necessarily agree with another person's opinion of a situation, we can still acknowledge their feelings about it. Everyone is entitled to feel the way they feel. It's not our place to tell someone how he/she should feel. How one person feels about rain doesn't negate how another person feels about it. Placing judgment on what's right and wrong when it comes to feelings only strengthens barriers.

Squash Fear

To build empathy, fear must be taken out of the equation. Judging someone's feelings is an act of fear. And its result is often even greater fear. Fear has its place, and is important to our basic survival, but in the instance of building empathy, it can seriously wipe out all hope of building common ground in a relationship.

By considering these factors of trust, you'll be better equipped to expand your relationships with your employees and allow for more real, in-depth, truthful discussions where viewpoints are expressed in an open, nurturing environment.

How to Train Staff to Build Trust with their Clients

Trust is the single most important component in relationships. Educate your staff on these essential actions that will help build loyalty and a formidable trust between them and their clients:

Be Present

When working with clients, be right there in the moment with them. Clients want to feel like they are the only people your staff wants to be talking with at that moment in time.

They want to be assured that their stylists are not thinking about dinner, about soccer practice or about the line of other clients waiting to be serviced. Make eye contact and ask questions.

Read Body Language

Body language is the secret language that communicates far more than our voices ever will. Our voices may say one thing, but our body language could be saying a totally different tale. One thing to remember is that body language rarely lies. If a client says yes to that warm brown shade a stylist wants to place over her brassy highlights, but her hands are clenched under her legs and all the color has washed from her face, it's obvious that she really doesn't want to become a brown headed woman just yet. Acknowledge her hesitation so she feels at ease and understood.

Remain True to Word

To build trust, a stylist must keep commitments. If a stylist promises to service someone and have her ready to go by a certain time, make sure that promise is realistic and kept. Breaking promises just diminishes hard earned value. Educate staff to only commit to those things that they are confident they can complete.

Be Honest

Trust is built from honesty, from admitting mistakes and from living up to the responsibilities of actions. When people have strong ethics, they are likely to receive more referrals. Clients will have full faith in their skills and be fully engaged in future business dealings.

LEAD WITH INTEGRITY

I've had all types of bosses in my life, and the ones who stand out as exceptional are always the ones who acted with full integrity.

Just like most people, I'd find it difficult to follow a person who wavers on principles and who can easily dismantle her opinions for the sake of someone else's. Employees crave stability and consistency from their leader.

When employees know with utmost certainty that you've got their backs regardless of the strain that is placed on them, they will take notice and go that extra mile for you.

Integrity brings out the best in people. When times get tough, your employees will look to you for guidance. By consistently providing solutions that support them, respect them, and help them work at their optimal level, you're helping them be the best they can be.

Integrity offers a freedom to soar. If your staff members know that the ground under their feet is solid, you will grant them the gift of freedom to soar without limits. This type of freedom is what offers the potential to take businesses to their next levels.

Effective Management Summary List:

- Provide an employee guidebook
- Conduct biannual performance reviews with the understanding of keeping a steady line of communication open year round
- Set goals and let them be involved in this process
- Create individualized and team incentive programs
- Conduct monthly staff meetings
- Be courteous and respectful when offering constructive criticism
- Assess training needs and provide assistance when appropriate
- Set an example by following your own rules

Chapter Four – Standing Out in the Crowd

The will to win, the desire to succeed, the urge to reach your full potential... these are the keys that will unlock the door to personal excellence. - Confucius

DEFINE YOUR BRAND

A guiding principle in marketing is to have an outstanding, definable brand that represents who you are and what you do well. It's finding a niche that reaches far beyond the generic, bland vanilla. It's going for real flavor so that when people indulge in your product, it dances on their tongue just as the popular Rocky Roads or Praline Supremes would. To stand out amongst the competition a brand has got to focus in on a clear demographic.

Chloe and I chatted about this very subject one hot afternoon as we sipped Ginger Ale on the salon's front porch swing.

"My niche was bridal parties," she said to me. "I decided I was going to be the best at this. My girls and I were prepared to travel to hotels, houses, and backyard patios if that's what it took. But, the phone hardly ever rang with a bride-to-be taking me up on this incredible service. I still don't get it."

"That was really specialized," I told her. "Do you think that maybe there weren't that many brides getting married to support your niche?"

To this she took a thoughtful sip and shrugged. "Who knows?"

Too narrow of a niche can do the opposite of a carefully defined one. Focusing just on brides may deter anybody who is not getting married or involved in that type of event from ever stepping foot in your salon.

Myers suggests that a new business owner be careful of focusing on something this specialized as a main brand. "It can still be part of your brand mix. You can gear your messaging to imply that it's your specialty, but you also want to be inclusive of people outside of that demographic. Deciding on your niche will take some upfront discovery research to determine if there is, indeed, a demand to support it."

So, bottom line is that whatever your niche is, you want to include that in your brand identity and positioning messaging. You don't want people to guess what your salon is about. You want them to understand who you are from your business card, to your window displays, to the products you sell, and to the manner in which your staff presents themselves. Brand is that constant link to your identity that is woven into every detail.

So in Chloe's case, she could've specialized in bridal styling, but a more successful branding strategy could've been hair color. This has more broad appeal, eliciting the interest of the masses, including brides! This would've given her a niche market without excluding the tangent population of the bridal parties. Her brand would've been taken up to a higher level. Many people seek out salons that are exceptional at coloring. This service is something that is of value and something that clients will most likely be willing to pay top dollar for because obviously the margin of error with that kind of service is high.

So, whatever your area of expertise is going to be, you want to make sure clients *get it*. Short of standing on the top of your building with a megaphone and shouting out to the world what you have to offer, you want clients to understand your value and position before they even step foot into your salon's front door.

IDENTIFY YOUR CORE DEMOGRAPHIC

One of the most effective ways to build a larger client base is to decide the clientele you wish to serve and then build a strong brand identity around them. So if you want to appeal to young professionals, chances are your stock shelves are not going to have purple and blue hair dye and wacky, tacky hair gels. Your service list will most likely feature spa pedicures or dimensional hair coloring over eyebrow piercings.

Once you know the clientele you wish to target, then you'll need to appeal to them. Attracting your core demographic depends largely on the ability to actually provide appropriate services, and doing it well.

Assess Your Target Market:

- Gender, age, income, lifestyle
- Who else offers this service?
- What is your unique selling point? Is it products, services, methods, your reputation, your training?

CREATING BRAND APPEAL

Think of a brand as the clothes, the makeup, the shoes, and the hairstyle of a person. A person wearing a pretty dress, shiny, new sandals, delicate makeup, and smooth, freshly cut hair has an air of sophistication. Another person dressed in worn jeans, a white tee shirt with an old ketchup stain, old sneakers and a neck overgrown with hair has an air of mega casualness. Each carries a different look, feel, and personality.

The same is true of a business brand. Each has its own distinct personality. A salon targeting affluent clients should have a look and feel that appeals to this market. They should leave the tacky colors and head-banging music to the salon around the corner who appeals to the wild and bold. Instead, this salon should dress their salon walls in soft hues with fancy finishes, place lively greenery in the corners, play soft jazz music, and serve chilled beverages adorned with fresh fruit. Everything from the front door, to the light switch covers, to the bathroom, and to the magazines on the reception area tables should spell out a first class personality. The brochures, business cards, and logos should all compliment the look and feel. The ads you place should reflect your salon's unique charm, including the words, the type font, and the images you use. Everything should match.

If you're targeting affluent clients, they will expect a high level of service where staff bends over backwards to create an ultimate experience. They may want to drink fine teas in fancy tea cups, eat gourmet scones and bite-sized sandwiches, and enjoy classical music while they browse your collection of Parisian art magazines. Proper branding includes setting a stage that caters to your demographic.

Another element of creating brand appeal is your position statement. A position statement is that over-arching principle for the entire marketing strategy. The marketing strategy sets the initial stage for all brand position planning. The goal in the beginning of this planning stage is to create messaging that's based on the key attributes of your services. If you don't have proper messaging, your brand falls short.

It's imperative to know your target clients so you can speak in terms they'll understand and respect. If you don't know how to speak to them, you may speak down to them. You may speak in more professional terms rather than laymen's terms. You may not speak to their lifestyle. For example, you might be talking about services that can be provided during the lunch hour when they don't even have to work for a living! Proper planning will help prevent wasted efforts and create more managed execution.

Salon uniforms are another element of branding. Uniforms set the first impression. What do you want a client's first thought to be about your salon? Professional? Chic? Stylish? Colorful? Artsy? All of the above? Branding requires consistent messaging, and nothing says consistency like the identifying force of a uniform. Uniforms cannot only establish brand, but they can also confirm professionalism and build trust subconsciously.

SUMMARY OF BRANDING ELEMENTS

- Consistent messaging (highlight the benefits and feelings your brand offers)
- Team members (attitude, personality, skill level)
- Color (warm, wild, tranquil, earthy, etc.)
- Sound (jazz, pop, hip-hop, funk, nature, loud, soft, etc.)
- Smell (earthy, incense, perfume, nails, chemical treatments, etc.)
- Décor (fun, trendy, comfortable, practical, wood, metal, etc.)
- Uniforms (apron, salon logo, clean and crisp, lab coat, consistent color, etc.)
- Products (top of the line, economical, exclusive, etc.)

CREATE A STYLE GUIDE

To create consistency in delivery of your brand message, establish guidelines for things like writing style on your website, ads and other promotional materials, and logo and color use.

SAMPLE STYLE GUIDE

Salon 123's Sample Style Guide

Typographic Guidelines:

Type: Salon 123's typographic identity is visible across many applications, including print ads, brochures and business stationary, electronic displays on the website, HTML emails, newsletters, and blogs.

To communicate in a consistent tone, the following type selections have been made to best represent the voice of Salon 123:

Headers: Garamond for all headlines

Text: Times New Roman

Sub Heads: Garamond Bold

Basic Design Elements:

- Chocolate Brown: Accent Color in all print and electronic formats
- White Space: Ample white space should be present in every layout.

- Logo: Logo must remain at its set ratio of three inches in width to one inch in height. When resized, this ratio must stay intact so that it is not stretched or morphed. The logo can only be in its true color of chocolate brown, or if placed on a dark background, it must be all white. The logo's typeface is Palatino Linotype, and its tag line is Times New Roman italics.

ANALYZE YOUR COMPETITION

To stand out from the crowd, one of the most critical questions that you need to ask yourself when planning is whether or not there is a demand for what you have to offer? If you're set to cut and style children's hair, then it would be wise not to set up shop in a retirement community. If you're targeting families, you might want to avoid Yuppieville.

Let's just say for the sake of example that you did find the perfect spot for your new trendy urban salon that caters to the brave at heart who enjoy fashion runway styles. The building is gorgeous. A metro runs parallel to the location. There are a few funky restaurants within walking distance, serving chilled tofu rolls, sushi, and seaweed smoothies. You think, "How could I turn down this gem?" And, I might be in your ear shouting, RUN! RUN! RUN!

If someone had been shouting this in Chloe's ear prior to her skipping into her new salon holding her new shiny key, she might've saved herself lots of headaches. What Chloe failed to see was that within a five-mile radius of her adorable new shop were about a hundred other adorable shops just like hers.

When you are planning your business, don't underestimate the power of location, location, location. A true gem is a place in an underserved community with an unmet need or gap in services. Realizing that there could be a demand for services that is not being provided is obviously more applicable to a smaller community than to a bigger city because it's a demographic numbers game. You want numbers on your side. You want people to NEED you. A little competition is good, but not when you're stepping on each other's toes and vying for the same air.

Make sure there is a demand for your services. Plan your location knowing that you have an exceptional and somewhat unique skill to bring to the market.

A lot of people neglect to do that in the beginning. They drive by an empty storefront, call the number, and a week later are painting walls and putting up their logo in the front window. They just go right after it without doing a competitive analysis.

CARVE OUT YOUR NICHE

Starting out on your journey to salon and spa ownership requires putting on a Sherlock Holmes hat, rolling up your sleeves, and really digging into the trenches of research to plan. This stage is when you size up the existing marketplace, identify a niche, discover an underserved community or service set, and then conjure up a way to market the right services to the right people at the right time and the right place. Successful market segmentation is taking all of this and using the right messaging and tone so that it's meaningful and relevant.

If you're trying to attract women aged thirty-five to fifty-five, offering a prom special that includes a complimentary manicure with an updo is not going to get you a salon full of your target population.

Understanding who your demographic is and realizing that the unique skills and services that you can provide in your community are going to be appealing to a specific demographic, is paramount. And it doesn't have to be really narrow. In other words, you don't necessarily have to go after just one segment. It could be, say, women eighteen to thirty-five years of age who are affluent, who are middle income or who are single or married. You just need to understand your different targets and that each one is unique and approachable in different ways.

In understanding this principle, your return on investment is going to be higher because you may be able to market and advertise less if you're doing it correctly.

You can have primary and secondary segments. Your primary may focus on color clients, while a secondary may focus on male cuts. Or you can also focus on individual services or packages of services that you can provide to even more secondary segments.

You just need to be strategic and thoughtful in your planning so you are streamlining your process.

Myers cited for an example, "Say with one of your ancillary services you are going to be appealing to men between the ages of forty and sixty. You can create a working campaign around that segment, funding ten percent of your marketing dollars towards it, so that's another source of revenue. As a word of caution, you're probably not going to want to include any marketing messaging towards services that appeal to this segment if they are not part of your larger target demographic."

OFFER THE RIGHT SERVICE

Many salons make the mistake of not understanding the psyche of affluent consumers. For instance, many might believe that affluent people spend their days shopping and tossing fifty dollar bills around like they were pennies. The truth is they can be frugal and discriminate with how they spend. Many affluent consumers expect more for their money in terms of service. The extra little touches of providing them with cucumber water as they're waiting to be serviced go a long way with them. They would much prefer drinking water out of a real glass over a disposable Dixie cup. They might adore being served on a tray. All these little extras add value and are what separate the mom and pop spots from the elite spas that know how to cater to this crowd. If they are going to spend their money, they want added values. You're not going to win this crowd over by waving coupons in their faces. But, offer them a slice of heaven while they are indulging in a service, and you've got their attention.

If your brand and your positioning are more high-end, you're setting an expectation. Therefore, these clients are buying and expecting a fuller and experience and a higher level of service. If they're going to be spending $150 on a haircut, they expect that they're buying a $150 haircut. They expect to get a full experience that's in line with who they are. For somebody else, a $150 haircut experience would be the latest and greatest, hippest, and coolest. Someone receiving this brand messaging might expect loud current music, stylists sporting pink extensions, and wacky, tacky styling products for their spiky, messy new dos. Make the experience match your brand. Be sure to position your offerings accurately whether they are affordable, luxury high-end, trendy, or ultra conservative.

Meet the expectation. If you're offering a luxury spa manicure, don't give a $10 manicure that someone can get in the clinic of a beauty school.

DEFINE WHAT MAKES YOU UNIQUE

A lot of small business owners make the mistake of not really understanding what it is they are really offering. When you welcome a client into your chair you are offering a service, sure, but even more than that, you are offering an experience.

Are you providing haircuts or are you providing an overarching feeling that the haircut gives to a client? This feeling, for example, can be one that emphasizes beauty, revitalization, affordability, or efficiency. It can be anything you want it to be. The important part is that you pinpoint what it is and brand your messaging around this feeling.

Let's say, for example, your offering is enrichment. Anything that touches the senses sticks. Sensory experiences attract themselves to that part of our brain that stimulates desire for more. So instead of thinking of your offerings as a haircut, a facial, or a pedicure, imagine the emotions that a client might tie to your salon if she felt she received not only a great haircut, but also a feeling of empowerment, of being enriched, and of freeing up her spirit?

That is branding.

If every time she thinks of your salon, she is rejuvenated with an intense feeling of enrichment, then you've got yourself the makings of a loyal customer. This feeling you're selling should be the core of your brand messaging. This message needs to be communicated in every detail, every word uttered, and every interaction. Whether you are answering a telephone call or waving goodbye as your newly enriched client leaves the salon, do so with this branding message in mind.

A salon experience that is very soothing, aesthetically pleasing, beautiful, and upscale offers sensory experiences way beyond the inch of hair that falls to the floor. When this client emerges out onto the street, she not only feels beautiful, but she also feels empowered and lifted because you offered her this pampering experience. That feeling will live on long after her freshly trimmed ends will.

Ask yourself what makes you unique to your target? Is it that you offer a tranquil environment focused on Feng Shui? Or maybe all your products and services are organic? Or maybe it's that your salon is fueled by a clean energy source like a windmill? Or maybe you cater to a male clientele. Or perhaps your salon is charitable and donates a portion of proceeds annually?

MEASURE YOUR SUCCESS

Developing a Return on Investment (ROI) understanding is so important when it comes to market penetration. Most small business owners without a clear idea of how to market effectively just sort of wing this wide-open field. They are the ones who just try something for the sake of taking some form of action. They are likely to toss an ad in the paper and see what happens without properly crafting the ad for maximum response. They are the ones who shrug if it doesn't work and either say, *print ads don't work* or they say *well that didn't work, so let's try a banner ad somewhere online.* If these people only realized there is a better way to measure effectiveness of advertising! Wouldn't they be surprised to realize that there really is! It's called – ROI.

Industry standard response rates that are used for traditional marketing channels can help us predetermine our return on an investment. For example, Myers points out, that the standard response rate from direct mail is typically three to four percent. Knowing that ahead of time, when going into a direct mail campaign, you would understand that to get ten new people in your door you'd need to mail to at least 3,000 names.

Quantifying and measuring your responses in this way will help you determine where you should be focusing your marketing budget dollars for future campaigns. If you send out 3,000 postcards and only get one person coming in the door from it, chances are your list isn't targeted correctly. So, you may decide to try a new list, create a greater call to action, or spend differently. Or maybe it's not the direct mail piece that's the issue, but an internal issue instead. Perhaps you discover that people are in fact calling up to inquire more about the postcard offer but your receptionist is the one turning them away with her attitude or her lack of knowledge about the incentive. In other words maybe she's not doing her job to get them in the door, in which case, you'll need to evaluate if she needs additional training or a friendly nudge out the door.

You want to look at how much it is costing you to advertise and what is your rate of return on this advertising investment. If it's not panning out, cut your losses and try a new measurable approach. The critical point here is to measure every marketing tactic you try. Be strategic in your approach! Otherwise, you could be wasting valuable dollars in areas that aren't worth a penny and missing out directing those dollars to an area that could produce multiple streams of revenue.

Chapter Five
Providing Exceptional Customer Service

As a single footstep will not make a path on the earth, so a single thought will not make a pathway in the mind. To make a deep physical path, we walk again and again. To make a deep mental path, we must think over and over the kind of thoughts we wish to dominate our lives. - Henry David Thoreau

BE CONSISTENT

Want to know the biggest secret of successful businesses? It's one that, if practiced repeatedly, will seriously get people smiling and walking through your door over and over and over again. It's one that, unfortunately, way too many businesses don't pay enough attention to it. Come close, real close and I'll reveal the golden rule that no business will ever want to ignore because to do so could spell a downward spiral so dangerous, your head might spin out of control.

BE CONSISTENT!

Imagine for a moment that you are a client coming into a salon for the first time. The welcoming receptionist blows you away as she sweetly greets you with a genuine smile and offers you a magazine and a cup of tea. She makes the tea perfectly, adding two teaspoons of raw sugar and a sprig of mint. As you sip your tea, you're soothed by pleasant jazz music and the delightful scent of freshly cut flowers. As soon as you are finished with your tea, the receptionist is right there to ask you if you'd enjoy a refill, to which you kindly reply *no thanks*.

And then, your new stylist arrives. Her hair is smooth as glass, her face manicured to perfection. She shakes your hand and guides you to her station where she drapes you in a colorful cape and dazzles you with her empathetic, listening ear. Finally, someone who gets you, who understands your natural curly hair, and who promises to give you a style you can comfortably walk away with and maintain yourself. Oh, yes, your wish has been granted! She expertly trims your hair, citing techniques like they were secret recipes, and the whole time you feel like you're the only person in the world who matters. When she completes your style, you look in that mirror and are in awe of her magic.

This will be the first time you can go shopping after a trim and not have to run home to style it yourself. You feel beautiful and enriched! You make your next appointment with her and leave declaring you will tell every single person you know what a great stylist she is.

Fast-forward six weeks. You are beyond excited to visit your friendly, talented stylist. You walk up those front steps and through that shiny red door. You can practically smell fresh lilies and feel the contagious smile you know you'll find on that friendly receptionist. This time, though, she rolls her eyes and wags her finger at you, mumbling something about being right with you. She's irritated at the caller on the phone, even snaps at her. You sit and grab your own magazine this time. She ends the call on a huff and doesn't look up at you. Finally, you go up to her and let her know you are waiting for Barb. She snaps at you saying Barb's running behind. You sit back down, beaten slightly from her tone. You are craving that cup of tea with the mint sprig but don't dare ask for it. You look around. No one is drinking tea or eating cookies this time. In fact, everyone is bowed into a magazine, probably afraid of the wrath happening at eye level.

You wait your turn, which ends up being thirty minutes. Barb emerges, frazzled. Her hair is frizzy and in a ponytail. It resembles a rat's nest. Her eyeliner is smudged, and she looks like she's ready to crash. Her white apron is stained black. She manages a weak smile and complains about her busy day and the fact that there are no towels in the back. She rushes you to the sink without bothering to drape you in a colorful cape or ask how your last trim was. She bangs your head around the sink bowl like it's a dishrag. Then, she sits you in the chair and starts cutting. She cuts and cuts and before you know it, she's smothering gel on your hair and whisking you towards the receptionist.

You're practically in tears now. So much for meeting your friends out for dinner right away. You need to go home immediately and wash your hair, which, as far as you can tell, is now one inch longer on the right side.

Doesn't take a rocket scientist to guess whether you will ever go back there.

How critical do you think clients are about their experience? Do you think they measure one visit against the other? You bet they do. I don't care if you are Vidal Sassoon or Paul Mitchell, if you are not consistent in your service, the client won't be coming back. Maintaining a quality of service throughout, and not just in the beginning, is, and always will be, a catalyst to bigger and better things in your future. You can't afford to be great one moment and suck the next. Clients won't have it. You can offer someone a positive experience ten times and mess up once, and guaranteed, that one time is all they will remember and judge you on.

It can be so tempting for a new business that has reveled in great press, exceptional reviews, and high return rates to get lax and say 'okay we've made it.' But, this is when you need to punch it into high gear and maintain your reputation. Most businesses are on their best behavior in the beginning. Employees are trained, motivated and fresh from the outside world. They are eager to grow with you. Then, complacency and familiarity set in. This is where the real danger lurks. This is when you need to step up and work that much harder to keep the momentum going, keep it fresh, and keep it fun and rewarding.

There is a mantra that successful business owners possess and that is: Provide great service all of the time. The customer should always know what to expect when she walks in your front door[3]. She should never be negatively surprised, wonder if your staff members are having a good or a bad day, or how her hair is going to turn out. Will I get a good cut or one that I have to go home and fix because Sally's boyfriend called her a name?

Every service your salon and spa provides should be given the same level of attention to detail. Whether your clients are coming in for a massage, pedicure, eyebrow wax or body wrap, they should always expect great service and receive it. The second that changes, your clients will drop off and go somewhere else where their expectations can be better met.

Customer service is an area where it's imperative to exercise the greatest level of attention. You may provide great service in terms of the stylist and her talents, but you may lose clients, even those clients who have been loyal for a while, if they get a bad customer service experience. All it takes is one time.

Loyalty can be broken at any time. Just because somebody has been loyal for years, doesn't mean that one bad event or experience, is going to keep him from seeking a better service at a different salon. Constantly being aware of the relationship factor will serve you well.

GET INTERACTIVE

If you make it easy for clients to give feedback, they will. Whether positive or negative, feedback is constructive as long as you take it to heart. If a client loved her experience you want to know so you can do more of this. If she was mistreated, you need to know so you can rectify and offer her a solution.

Customer satisfaction needs to be a top priority for obvious reasons, and it can also help motivate staff. If they know they are positively affecting someone's life, they will most likely respond with even more of the great service they provided to get such a rave review. To capture such feedback, post your email information on your receipts. Or provide a client feedback box on your website. Or send follow up email surveys to clients who recently visited.

Customer Service Markers:

- Salon and stations are tidy and sanitary
- Client is greeted warmly and quickly
- Client is offered a beverage
- Product is clearly displayed and easy to browse
- Price list is clearly displayed in a brochure
- Service is always timely
- Clients are rewarded for loyalty through special added value promotions

.

Chapter Six – Increasing Profits

Determine never to be idle. No person will have occasion to complain of the want of time who never loses any. It is wonderful how much may be done if we are always doing. -
Thomas Jefferson

You could be the greatest salon this side of the Atlantic Ocean and it wouldn't matter one bit if no one knew you existed. This is why every salon needs a marketing budget if you want to target your ideal clients and entice them into your salon's loving arms.

Promoting a salon might seem intimidating to those who have never delved into the seemingly big, scary world of marketing. But, it can be truly fun and rewarding. Sure, it requires some creative ingenuity and a willingness to step outside of your comfort zone. Without stretching a bit, you're not going to grow all that much. And, as a business owner, growing should be your number one priority aside from enjoying yourself in the process.

CROSS PROMOTE

Want to save money and have instant access to your target audience? Cross promoting with other companies who target that same market is extremely cost-effective. You share in the cost or, better yet, barter for services. Seek out opportunities with local businesses where you can get discounts or free prime ad placement for exchange in services.

Myers says that crafting a deal like this is going to require some negotiation skills in the sense of coming up with creative ways you both will benefit. Reciprocity, which is the act of reciprocating one action for another, is a beautiful thing!

Getting out there and talking with other businesses may be uncomfortable for some. When it comes to your business success, though, fear needs to take a back seat. You have to push forward with your goal in mind. In this case, the goal is to get word out that you offer these fabulous services, and to get that word out at a low cost or for free.

Myers says, "You can't be afraid to take this action. I'm surprised at how many people are afraid to ask, and what I always say to them is that it never hurts to just pose the question. If you do it in a way that's not offensive and that is mutually beneficial, there's no downside. You're simply helping each other spread the word about your valuable businesses."

Another tactic can be to ride the coattails of existing mature brands that already appeal to your target demographic. For example, let's take a peripheral market like hotels. Suppose your salon and spa is located within a reasonable distance to a hotel that matches your core demographic clientele. You could create some sort of promotional package that you offer exclusively to the hotel guests. Or you could create a line of shampoo and conditioner that the hotel offers guests. You can create customizable packaging with your logo and salon information and house these in a small basket on the vanity sink. Next to it can sit a tastefully designed card with an incentive to purchase more products from your website.

Because the hotel has already built up a client base with the ideal clients you wish to target, you're riding on their brand and on the trust their clientele ties to their brand. The hotel guests are automatically going to believe in you because the hotel they admire is recommending you as someone they trust. This strategy of riding on the coattails of a mature brand can prove to be a really important strategy for any new business trying to create a brand of their own.

Another example of co-branding is thinking up themed packages and connecting with obvious businesses in that themed circuit. So, maybe your core demographic consists of families with teenagers. Perhaps you create a package and co-promote it with a limousine company, a flower company, a tuxedo rental store and a dress shop. Create a prom package where all the businesses work together to promote. This will open up your business to all sorts of new clients that fit your demographic, widening your exposure with the existing audiences of each business.

Or say your core demographic is comprised of young professionals who work in the city. You could promote an elegant dinner and theatre themed package. Or maybe a package that promotes a romantic getaway where the couple gets special rates at the hotel nearby, romantic dinners for two at a special rate, and the wife or the girlfriend/spouse gets pampered beforehand at your salon and spa for a couple of hours that afternoon. The businesses involved bring it all together, do all the footwork for the scheduling, and create a full experience that'll have people bragging for months. The goal of this concept is to share in the cost of promoting, share your exposure, and share your audience.

CREATIVE PACKAGE IDEAS

Romantic Getaway - Team up with a piano bar and a luxury car service. The couple starts out with a couple's massage, mud bath and primping of hair and makeup (for the lady), then a luxury car driver takes them to a romantic piano bar.

Girl's Night Out - Team up with a local restaurant, a limo company, and a local nightclub. The girls start out getting their nails, hair and makeup perfected, take off in a limo to eat dinner, and then go out on the town.

Wine and Dine - Team up with a local winery and an antique car rental company. Offer a luxury ride to the spa, offer pampering services, and then an afternoon touring a winery.

Sun and Fun - Team up with a local golf club and create a package that starts out with a round of golf, lunch, and then ends in pedicures and massages to relax achy muscles.

The Birthday Escape - Team up with a local teahouse. Birthday girl and a guest enjoy relaxing treatments and top their day with teas, scones, sandwiches and fruit-filled tarts.

OFFER QUALITY RETAIL PRODUCTS

A hugely missed revenue opportunity in many salons is in the retail center. Retail is one easy way to increase revenue exponentially from your current clientele. Selling is intimidating and uncomfortable. That's why you never want your staff to look at retail as selling, but rather friendly suggesting.

As a stylist, you have a client's full attention while she is in your chair. She comes to you because she needs you. She relies on you for guidance, education, and to ensure you don't let her walk out that door looking like a fool. While she is in your chair and you are listening to her talk on and on about her cat's constant need to scratch its paws against her leather couch or the great job her ten-year-old son is doing in his math class, you have many opportunities to turn that conversation into something more fruitful for you both. People love to learn. They love to feel enriched. They love the idea of gaining insight. Gift them with this.

By simply talking out loud about what you are placing in their hair, you are informing them to make better decisions. You are offering them information that can benefit them. Go one step further and actually place that product in the palm of their hands, and allow them to smell it, to feel it, to place it in their hair. By doing this you have made them curious and made them emotionally attached.

When you walk them out to the reception area and hand them a bottle of the cream you applied to their hair, a cream that is making them feel radiant, you are making the decision easier for them. If they're not committed to purchasing right then and there, write your recommendations down for them. Then, offer to them that if they buy all three of the products you recommend at that moment, you will give them one for half price. They will stop and think. You've piqued their interest. You are not selling them anything. You are informing them. You have engaged their sense of touch, smell, sight, and hearing. You have just increased their ticket by doing what you'd be doing anyway, talking with them and guiding them. Now, when they go home and style themselves, they can get great results and feel fabulous instead of tacky and sticky from their drugstore products.

ADD VALUE

Nothing screams RUN louder than a person we don't trust with a pair of scissor, nail clippers, or hot wax. You can cast your net well across the state of Texas and if people don't trust you, they're not going to listen. You may as well be singing to a pile of rocks.

To produce a moneymaking machine, one where the phone is literally ringing itself silly and your appointment book is so far booked into the future that you need a computer system with multiple year capabilities just to keep appointments straight, you need to build TRUST and CREDIBILITY. Once these two attributes are earned, your profit potential is endless.

To maximize your profits, aim to turn small ticket items into bigger ones. Train your staff to turn haircuts into highlights, colors, facials, massages, waxes, or nail clients, too. Your job as professionals is to educate, and get clients to count on them to educate. The word upselling may come to mind when you think of 'talking clients into' something new and beyond what they requested. When a client is upsold by a new stylist to them, it can be off-putting and abrasive if not presented correctly. And, if not executed artfully, can even backfire on you.

This is when confidence and trust come into play. When you've built up the credibility and trust, clients will listen and rely on your guidance.

Myers suggests, "While a client is sitting under the dryer, you can suggest a complimentary paraffin hand treatment, the newest technique you just learned at a convention, or offer up a mini complimentary add-on service to get them hooked."

Your staff has now built up that trust factor by showing clients instead of just telling them. Clients are experiencing the effects and the benefits of the services. Now they're hooked. Next thing you know, you're booking them for two or three additional services when they come in for their trims.

A misconception that many small business owners have is that they look at the cost of these complimentary or discounted services and they focus on the money they lost from not charging. They might be thinking, "Well, gosh, I'm giving away $20, $30, even $50 worth of services" instead of looking at this action more strategically as a potential future gain. A client who used to get only $300 worth of services a year is now spending well over $600 as a result of offering her this irresistible trial.

A smart move would be to offer these trials to clients who will spread the word. Seek out these types of clients, the ambassador types with a verbose personality who isn't afraid to give her opinion. Before long, you'll have an army of salespeople selling for you without taking a salary! This kind of free advertising spreads like a fire in dry leaves.

You give them a $50 service for free, and they in turn bring you in ten new clients who want to experience the bliss their friend bragged she just had. The exponential return on that over time is limitless.

GET PEOPLE TALKING

This segues nicely into word-of-mouth marketing. It is so cost-effective and useful in today's business. People, especially women, pay attention to the opinions of friends, families, colleague, and even people they don't know. We see this all the time with all these feedback systems online.

The fact worth pointing out here is that feedback of any kind, from anybody that seems to be reliable, is more believable than any promises you might make in your advertisement. Consumers are so much savvier now. They realize that marketing and advertising is often simply insulated promises. It's just marketing.

Get people talking - word-of-mouth, word-of-mouth, word-of-mouth. Myers says, "I cannot say that enough, especially with women. Women are natural word-of-mouth marketers. They are the key information seekers, decision makers, and influencers. So, if they have a great experience, they are going to tell people about it. They are your unpaid sales people."

CREATE A LOYALTY PROGRAM

Here's a great tool for testing response rates, a loyalty program. Call it something catchy, like Spalicious and create adorable credit card–sized member cards. Track their purchases, their services, and frequency. Run specials for Spalicious members and promote them in different ways. Perhaps you have a new service you want to push, test it on your Spalicious members. Be sure to measure the promotion's effectiveness.

Take this a step further and push those services that aren't popular, the ones that you want to make more popular. Perhaps it's waxing, manicures, or spray tanning. As Spalicious members, they'll get to add on this service to an existing one for five or ten dollars. They try it out and love it, then all of a sudden are flying in and out of your salon doors every week to get it done again and again and again.

GET PEOPLE EXCITED

Reward people for their purchases by offering a raffle. Set it up so that every two months you are raffling off a new gift.

To be entered, all a client needs to do is spend twenty dollars or more on retail product. Then, every two months, you draw a name and announce the winner. They come in, you snap a picture of them beaming and excited, and you post this for all to see. Maybe the raffle is a gift basket full of their favorite four products, or maybe it's a complimentary skin care treatment, or better yet, maybe every so often they can choose a charity and you donate a set amount to that charity in their name (this will also carry great free publicity with it).

REV UP SLOW TIMES

Thinking outside the box - a great way to publicize your offerings to newcomers and to beef up the slow moments is to offer happy hour. Play soft jazz music and serve chilled drinks for an hour during slowest times. Happy hour specials can include:

- Complimentary bottle of nail polish with the purchase of a manicure
- Complimentary brow wax with the purchase of a lip wax
- Complimentary hand massage with the purchase of a pedicure

Or, turn your salon into a knitting club haven. Invite knitters to knit and socialize and get upgraded spa pedicures at the same time. Serve fruity drinks and cookies and you'll be the hosting hero.

Or consider a happy hour based around an art show. Invite local artists to display their art. Clients can browse and receive special deals on retail products just for showing up.

GET SOME PRESS ON YOUR SIDE

If you're looking to spread your net further out into the community, press is an inexpensive way to get word out to the masses. A word about press releases: Make it newsworthy! Perhaps you're donating a portion of proceeds to a charity, having a book drive, or offering free massages to cancer survivors (you get the picture).

Press releases get picked up by newspaper editors, television stations, radio stations, and website editors who see value in it for their readers. It is not about sales or promotions. Think community. The goal is to create a professional impression, one that makes people want to be a part of your mission. You gain credibility and are exposed to a whole lot of people interested in what you're doing.

When writing a press release, it can be helpful to have a set of questions on hand to ask yourself so that its focus remains newsworthy.

PR QUESTIONNAIRE

- What do you want to announce?
- Why is this news significant?
- What does this news mean to your business?
- If you could tell your key prospects and customers just 3 things about this news and why it is important, what would they be?
- Who are the key people involved in the decision from your side and any other relevant parties? Do you have any quotes to provide from these people? (List specific names and title, and make sure spelling is correct; you should also obtain approval from any parties you wish to quote prior to distribution.)
- What industries is your news relevant to?
- Which publications do you believe will find this news relevant?
- If the reader of your press release could link to 3 places on your website, where would they be?
- Anything else you'd like to share about this news?

PRESS RELEASE EXAMPLE

Salon 123 to donate 10% of retail product sales in March 2012 to The Jimmy Fund.

Baltimore, MD – February 5, 2014 – Salon Owner and Manager, Suzie Martin, has committed to donate 10% of retail product sales this March to <u>The Jimmy Fund</u>. The product lines involved are: Paul Mitchell, L'Anza, and Redken.

Since its founding in 1948, the Jimmy Fund has supported the fight against cancer in children and adults at Boston's Dana-Farber Cancer Institute, helping to raise the chances of survival for cancer patients around the world.

"I have a passion for helping others, especially those afflicted with cancer," Martin states. "I think it's important to give back to those who need help. It feels great, and it's something I'll remain committed to doing."

By purchasing products from Salon 123 in March 2014, patrons can help to support the pediatric community.

Salon 123 is located in Elkridge, MD, and welcomes new clients.

To learn more about The Jimmy Fund visit www.jimmyfund.org. To learn more about Salon 123, visit: www.insertwebsitehere.com

###

For more information: Suzie Martin | 443-555-5555

GIVE BACK

Everyone feels great when they've given a gift back to the community in one form or another.

People also rally behind organizations that stand for the greater good of others. Warm hearts and you've got loyal clients for a lifetime.

Create a monthly public relations campaign around some of these ideas and let the media know so they can share these heartwarming stories with the greater community:

Treat a soldier to a day spa package for her service to our country

Treat a cancer patient to an hour long massage

Have clients nominate a local hero who goes above and beyond for the sake of others, and treat her to a day at the spa

Team up with a local hospital and offer a package to an outstanding nurse

Chapter Seven – Getting Social - Online

*No matter how many goals you have achieved, you must set
your sights on a higher one. - Jessica Savitch*

If you are that unique person who doesn't have a Facebook
or Twitter account, this is what you need to do. Ready for
some pretty revolutionary advice? Here goes. Log onto a
computer, immediately, and get yourself a FREE account on
both of these sites. Those two steps will save you thousands of
advertising dollars and create more loyalty and opportunity
than any other generation of new business owners could've
ever achieved prior to the invention of these two social sites.
Why? Because virtually everyone is on board these moving
trains. And, if you engage correctly, creatively, and
professionally, you've got a true treasure of an engaged
audience at your fingertips.

FACEBOOK

Here's what you do. Create a fan page for your salon and spa. Get thirty people to 'like' it, and you can name it what you want. Otherwise you're stuck with some long strange name with lots of characters no one will ever be able to remember.

Once you've got your fan page appropriately named after your business, start promoting it and interacting. Post photos of the salon, the staff, a portfolio of styles, and info about product lines. Write notes with tips on everything from taming frizzy hair to choosing the right style to maintaining perfect skin health. To get people interacting, host a weekly product giveaway with a trivia question. All who answer correctly can be entered into a drawing and one winner per week is drawn and announced.

Toss in some promotions, incentives, specials, and you've got yourself free twenty-four hour access to your clients' eager eyes, and all of their friends, and their friends, and so on. Your goal is to get as many people as possible to 'Like' your fan page. Place this link in all of your ads, promotions, sponsorships, collateral, etc. Before long, you will have yourself one heck of a substantial following.

One word of advice that can't be stressed enough is consistency. Be consistent and timely with your postings. Schedule a post like you would a client in an appointment book. You must be present for engagement to work. Once a week post a special, a note, a question, or fun trivia. Anything to get people clicking and browsing your site.

Things to ask yourself as you create your posts:

- If I were scrolling my newsfeed and came across a similar post, would I 'like' it, comment on it, or share it?
- If this is a photo post, is it relevant and empowering enough to cause someone to engage with it?
- Does this post offer something valuable in terms of tips, information, or entertainment?

Some helpful posting tips:

- Use engaging copy, images and videos
- Be sure to add your website to each photo.
- Whenever possible, use original photography. If you use someone else's, be sure to obtain their permission.
- Try to keep your posts between 100 and 250 characters to get more engagement. Shorter, succinct posts are better received.

- Facebook pages has a tab for 'apps'. Place links to your other social media sites here (i.e. Twitter, Pinterest, YouTube, etc.).

- Create a conversation by asking for feedback, and responding to that feedback.

- Offer special deals through your Facebook page to encourage more 'likes'.

Facebook recommends that companies create a conversation calendar. Jot down a plan of what you'll say and when. This creates a sense of consistency across the board. Maybe one day you feature testimonials, another styling tips, and another product uses.

Schedule your posts ahead of time to keep to your plan.

Use your website link in your posts to drive website traffic.

BLOG

Go one step further and create a blog. This blog can offer exclusive deals to subscribers. Take that long list of fans and ask them to subscribe. Dangle an incentive in front of them so they have a really hard time refusing! Now, you have a targeted list to send direct communications, and you can start offering viral offers to them that can also be passed along to their friends that may not already be aware of your salon.

You can write your own blog, base it on the latest styles, trends, or even more personal stuff like *a day in the life at Bella Spa.*

Or if you aren't a writer, hire someone to write your blog. You can find them on freelance websites, or even by visiting relevant sites like beauty and healthcare where you may find the movers and shakers of bloggers.

Blogging is interactive. People can comment on yours, you can comment on theirs. If you search and find health and beauty blogs, comment on them. People following those blogs will then see you post and become curious and may follow your blog!

Another benefit is that oftentimes when you're blogging or someone is commenting on your blog or you're commenting on someone's blog, what happens is that the internet will take note and increase your search ranking - FOR FREE.

Bottom line is the more people talking about your salon, the better.

WHY A BLOG?

Build contacts:

Each website visitor is a potential client. Capture their email and you can communicate with them on a regular basis.

Out of sight, out of mind:

You want to be on your clients' minds so they don't forget about you. Give them a reason to come back time and again.

Form a trusting bond:

Ongoing communication can build trust over time, especially when you offer them professional tips and information.

Target promotions:

Easily let your blog subscribers know about upcoming deals that they won't want to miss.

HOW TO CREATE AN IDEAL BLOG

- Keep your headline under 6 words
- Hook readers in with a great opening paragraph that is anecdotal
- Use a featured image
- Subheads for scanning
- Keep content to the sweet-spot of 1,500-words
- Use a friendly interface. I like Wordpress. It offers easy-to-use tools, valuable plug-ins, opt-in subscriber form, and lots of templates.
- Be sure to link back to your website
- Encourage comments and engage with those who take the time to leave one.

TWITTER

When you sign up for a Twitter account, choose a user name that is unique and apropos to who you are. The trick with selecting a user name is to make who you are as a business obvious so people will 'follow' you based on their perceived value of what your tweets will offer. In other words, if your brand is centered around being coloring experts, then call yourself something to that effect so people searching Twitter will come across your profile.

So your account name is your business name, and your user name could be something like @color_expert or something to that effect. Too many people miss great opportunities to get noticed on Twitter simply because they use acronyms that no one would ever be searching for on Twitter (or remember).

Use hashtags when tweeting. Hashtags look like this #beauty, and they should be placed in your 140 character tweets. Anyone searching twitter for beauty related tweets will find yours.

There are two top-notch free Twitter applications that let you manage all your social media accounts in one place. They are Hootsuite and Tweetdeck. They both have similar benefits and are considered reliable and user-friendly. Which one to choose comes down to personal preference in regards to the look and feel of the application. Hootsuite does offer a few more bells and whistles that may or may not be critical for your purposes.

Both allow you to update your Facebook and LinkedIn account, create and manage twitter lists, keep up with trending events, follow topics with saved searches, and schedule tweets ahead of time.

HootSuite also allows users to view, manage, and post to WordPress. It has a tabbed browsing format and allows access to multiple windows within one browser. HootSuite offers two URL shortening options with Ow.ly and Ht.ly. And lastly, you can also track your 'favorites' and 'retweets' statistics.

Both are worth checking out.

A consist presence is key with Twitter.

Twitter moves fast, and if you're not posting daily, you're likely to get swallowed up in the masses.

Set up your tweets in the morning. Schedule them to go out every hour or two. Make them relevant to your business (i.e. show off your personality, offer tips, link to blog posts and relevant articles, post quotes, say something funny, post specials, etc.)

Ideally, you'll take some time and create a working spreadsheet of posts that you can copy and paste right into one of these applications. Keep adding to this spreadsheet, and recycle posts over time.

The goal with Twitter is to post stuff that you would retweet if you read it in your twitter feed. Also, add images to your posts to make them stand out.

You only get 140 characters per tweet. If your goal is to have people retweeting your posts, you want to make sure you stay under 100 characters so people can add a reaction to it if they choose.

Be sure to interact with your followers. If they mention you in a tweet, mention them back. If someone 'follows' you, be sure to follow up with a direct message thanking them and asking them an interactive, open-ended question that will strike up a lively discussion and hopefully pique their curiosity to visit your website for hair care tips and/or product deals. Something as simple as: Thanks for following! If you could ask one burning question about health and beauty, what would it be?

How to Get Followers

One simple strategy is to follow a set number of new people daily. A word of caution, be sure not to follow too many people at once. Twitter doesn't like this and they may suspend your account for short or long term. Be sure to read their terms and conditions. Based on their current terms and conditions, it seems that a safe number is ten to twenty followers a day. Follow people who are relevant to your business. Perhaps this is someone into fashion who reads

Glamour, someone who is a fan of a product line you offer, or someone who enjoys following the beauty trends of a leading fashion company. You can find them by visiting the pages of say Glamour, Matrix, and Ann Taylor Loft and searching their 'followers list'. Simply click on 'follow' next to their name. If they follow you back, follow up with that open-ended question above. And be sure to visit their tweets and interact when possible.

Another way to gain new followers is by holding contests.

Here's a fun easy way to get more buzz, more clients, and more of an online presence with existing clients. Ask your clients to tweet five words that describe their recent salon experience, and then they will be entered into a chance to win a prize, be it a free product or service.

To enter, have them follow some easy instruction such as:

- Follow you on Twitter
- Tweet five words describing their recent salon experience
- Include a catchy hashtag like #tweet4treats and then a mention of your salon (@salon123)

Be sure to include an expiration date, and then when this one is complete, create another campaign asking for them to describe something else.

Post this contest on your salon's Facebook page, on your website, on your blog, on posters in your salon, and on small cards that you can hand to your clients along with their receipt from that day's service.

Myers says, "I can't stress enough how valuable of a tool Twitter can be, especially if you sell retail on your site. Someone living across the country can purchase from you. This opens up a whole new level of income."

I'd be remiss if I didn't jump in here with a professional word of caution on selling retail online. As professionals, it's critical to uphold the integrity of professional hair care products by protecting against diversion (black market sales). The temptation might be there if someone calls your salon and orders bulk quantities of product. You've got yourself a willing customer who wants to fork over lots of money for lots of product. The threat to the professional hair care industry comes when these customers resell these bulk purchases on the black market.

Prevent diversion by limiting online sales to a certain, reasonable quantity for an individual.

YOUTUBE

YouTube is a creative way to get in front of a whole new audience, and to educate existing clients. Imagine if once a month, you post a new video that demonstrates how to blow out straight hair, how to braid, how create a messy updo, how to create smoky eyes, etc. How viral can you go? VERY VIRAL! Not only will this increase traffic to your site, but if you relevantly tag your videos and have those tags in the description field, it'll also increase your Search Engine Optimization (SEO). What this means is the higher your SEO is, the greater your chances are of showing up on Google searches when someone is searching for 'hair salon in xyz city' or 'online beauty products'.

Again, the purpose is to stay in contact with clients, build new interest, and if you sell retail online, to attract new retail sales (in a manner that doesn't support product diversion, of course!).

Build YouTube Subscriber List

- Create weekly videos to post.

- Craft contests that will encourage subscribing to and sharing your channel.

- Capture video from special events like weddings, proms, special packages, etc (with permission of course)!

INSTAGRAM

Instagram is the popular picture app. This neat app is a fantastic marketing tool.

Instagram allows you to create an air of personal touch between you and your clients. You get to showcase your personality! Pictures can be goofy, serious, dramatic, lively, anything you want them to be. Clients get a behind-the-scenes peek, and this creates a personal touch that stretches beyond the scope of the salon chair.

Another neat feature is that Instagram is connected to Facebook and Twitter. You can easily connect to all of your networks without added work.

Just as with all other social media programs, you have to stay active to continue to build and maintain your presence.

AFFILIATE MARKETING

Affiliate marketing is based on reciprocity. You allow other service providers and product manufacturers in similar or peripheral industries to advertise on your site and vice versa. Both of you will post an advertisement on each other's site that will provide a link that goes back to your respective site. Because this is reciprocation, there is no cost to either of you. You're basically riding the coattails of each other like in cross promotion.

GROUPONS AND LIVING SOCIAL

These two companies can be great for small businesses. The service they provide is highly effective and can deeply increase your targeted reach.

Groupon is a deal-of-the-day website that features discounted gift certificates usable at local or national companies.

Living Social is a local marketplace that features discounted gift certificates

At a Glance Benefits:

- They can bring in a large number of customers in a short amount of time.

- They can reach new audiences.

- No money is necessary upfront. Instead, these two companies only make money if you make money. So, instead of putting up large amounts of money to jumpstart a marketing campaign, LivingSocial and Groupon take a share of your profits. You only have to pay them if you get an increase in business.

Sounds like a win-win.

Cautionary note: Be sure your salon can handle a sudden influx of this discounted business.

WEBSITE

Yes, I know, this should really go without saying. You must have a website if you want to reach out to the masses and build your business to its fullest potential. There are many website templates and hosting packages available. All you have to do is a simple search and choices will appear.

There are some DIY sites to help you launch one yourself, and then there are the pros who can help you create a look of sophistication. Be sure to contract someone who will create a site you can maintain on your own after. There are some website consultants who will dazzle you with a beautiful site and charge you for each change you want to make later on. Avoid this type of situation at all times.

A good website consultant will work with you to create what you need, then train you on how you can maintain that going forward.

I highly recommend www.maximwebsites.com. They build your mobile responsive site, then you control it afterwards. They create websites that give you back-end access so you can control your content 24/7. They also provide tutorial videos and support when needed.

Websites serve many purposes: to educate, to welcome, to invite, to sell, to introduce, to entice, or to show off your appeal. I could go on for pages. The most important thing is that the website should reflect your brand and, on its simplest terms, be comprised of basic website necessities.

A website not only serves as a hub for all information about your salon, but it can also do things like offer retail products to people in and out of your geographic area and build you targeted lists. Every page on your site should be equipped with a subscriber widget that allows people to sign up for deals, information, and all things beauty. Once you build a sizable list, you can offer exclusive specials to these people, enticing them to buy, buy, buy from you!

Whether you are building your site yourself or having a professional build it for you, here are some technical things to keep in mind.

THINGS TO AVOID ON YOUR WEBSITE

- Dense copy blocks
- Complicated sentences
- PDF and "flip" publications
- Over-sized photos

THINGS TO CONSIDER ON YOUR WEBSITE

Images:

- Ensure all images are relevant to your salon and its offerings
- When naming images, use keywords as file names
- For search engine optimization, use dashes, not underscores, to separate each word in a phrase with a name
- Use descriptive ALT and TITLE attributes on all images
- Each image should be unique and should not use more than a dozen words in its description

Navigation:

- Ensure each page contains consistent navigation
- The navigation should indicate the current page
- Your navigation buttons should stand out from the rest of the content on your pages
- FAQ should be prominent in the navigation
- Navigation aids, such as site map, skip navigation link, or breadcrumbs should be used (accessibility)
- All navigation hyperlinks should work and not be broken

Basic Layout:

- Consistent site header/logo on each page
- Informative page title that includes the company name
- Page footer area — copyright, last update, contact e-mail address
- Site should have a balance of text/graphics/white space
- Home page should have compelling, interesting information above the fold at 1024x768
- Home page should download within 10 seconds on dial-up connection
- Let no paragraph run longer than 5 lines
- Keep every sentence as short as possible
- Every page on your website should include subheads and bullet points that quickly communicate the key points of the page in 5-seconds or less
- If you have many pages (more than 7 or 8), it may be best to organize them by category and have drop down menus
- Information should be easy to find (minimal clicks)
- Ensure content is free of typographical and grammatical errors

Fonts:

- Use sans-serif fonts
- Limit the number of fonts to 2 or possibly 3 standard font families

Links:

- Ensure meaning of link text is clear and each is unique.
- Each button/link should have a short name - preferably one word
- Captions should be provided for each audio or video file used (accessibility)
- Content provides links to other useful sites
- Avoid the use of "Click here" when writing text for hyperlinks, instead be obvious (i.e. list of services, contact us, for more tips)

Basic Design

- Use of different colors in page backgrounds/text is limited to a max of three or four colors plus neutrals
- Use color consistently
- Color should have good contrast with associated text
- Color should not used alone to convey meaning (accessibility)
- Use of color and graphics should enhance rather than detract from the site

EMAIL MARKETING

With your targeted list, you have access to a captive audience who has granted you permission to send them information electronically.

Send out monthly emails focused on upgrading services from standard to luxury as a reward for completing a survey, or referring a friend, or using a code in the email. You can email birthday gifts of a free product of their choice at their next visit. You can push an added service by offering a complimentary conditioning treatment when they mention your email.

Many HTML service providers offer templates. These make it easy to upload images and text. I love Mailchimp. There site is easy to use, robust, and affordable.

Keep in mind that you must stay in line with SPAM laws. Any reputable HTML service provider will offer subscriber widgets to correctly generate permission-based lists, provide easy to manage opt-outs, and allow you to track the success of each html email campaign. Keep your subscriber form simple, and be sure to thank each new subscriber and to communicate your respect for his or her privacy.

Chapter Eight – Maintaining Value

Set your sights high, the higher the better. Expect the most wonderful things to happen, not in the future but right now. Realize that nothing is too good. Allow absolutely nothing to hamper you or hold you up in any way. - Eileen Caddy

Price competition, we see it everywhere. Headlines pop out at us like clowns at a circus with deals of the century: *Get ten dollars off! Receive fifty percent off! Why pay top dollar when you can pay just five dollars!* The deals, *as irresistible as they can appear, beg the question: but* why? The cynic in me always thinks something must be wrong with this product or service if you have to discount it. Are you not able to make your sales quota? Are your stylists not talented so you have to discount? Is your haircut not really worth the full value so your only choice is to slash prices to get me in the door?

Okay so say I'm not really saying these things and I just want a cheap haircut? I go in, get a great cut at a discounted rate and love it. I book my next appointment and ask what the

117

real rate is. You tell me it's ten dollars more than what I just paid. If what lured me in the door was the cheap price, do you think I'm really going to come back and feel good about paying you almost double what I just did? Once I pay the discounted price, I don't want to pay full price again. You're messing with my brain!

Bottom line, when you discount, you cheapen your brand. Unless your brand is cheap prices, you should avoid this tactic.

MAINTAIN PERCEIVED VALUE

People will pay more for what they perceive is luxury or above and beyond the natural call of service. When you look at some of the high-end designers or products, they are not necessarily any better than any of the others. But, they are perceived to be. Take for example, Godiva Chocolates. Some may argue that their chocolate isn't any better than the chocolate products found in grocery store aisles. But, the perception is they are better because the rich brand, with its gold packaging, signifies that it is superb amongst ordinary chocolates. Give the gift of Godiva and the receiver will know you gave her quality. Rich brands like Godiva can charge more because they've built a perceived value into their brand that resonates deep within consumers' hearts.

So the trick to avoiding price wars is to outsmart the competitors. Don't play on their field. Create your own where they can't even compete. You can do this by brand appeal and also by offering added value to services, rather than discounting.

Be aware that when you engage in that cheapest price battle you are diminishing the brand's services.

OFFER A MINI-VERSION

Imagine you just attended a premiere educational event where you learned some of the latest and greatest skin care techniques that would knock the socks off your clients. You go back to the salon, fully charged with new info, dying to introduce your clients to these services that no one else can offer them because they are that new. You start promoting the newest facial with skin recharging capabilities far exceeding anything anyone has yet to see. You just know people are going to be banging down the double louver doors to your facial room to get this procedure done.

You know this because your clients have been begging you to cure their sun-laden skin. So, you hang the new flyers, post the great news on your website, blog about the great effects, and rave in your 140 characters on Twitter that this service is now available. And, no one calls.

Two weeks go by and not one client even feigns interest. Your dreams of increased revenue shatter like broken glass at your feet. You swore with the added service you'd be able to upgrade the facial chair to the luxury level and even have funds left over for your staff's incentive program. You start to push the service only to be thwarted with a fast shake of the head or, worse, a quick dash out the door.

No one is taking advantage of this great technique and you don't have a clue why. You think, geez, if only they could try it and see the proof. But no one is willing. They're opting for the basics.

Here is what you need to do in this case: go back and revisit your business plan. Is this new service aligned with your core demographic? Are you offering a service that far exceeds their pocketbooks? Or their time? Are you offering the latest and greatest, but marketing to a clientele that's not interested in it because maybe they are too traditional and don't give a darn about the latest and greatest? Have you branded yourself as a salon that is the best at quick treatments professionals can get on their lunch break? How have you positioned yourself and how can you reposition this service to fall within the perimeters you've set?

So maybe, let's say, if the demographic is in tune with the great benefits and are really interested but just don't have the time or the money to try it, meet them halfway – literally. Offer a mini service that is half the price and half the time and you both win. They get to experience the benefits, you get to realize added dollars, and eventually, once they're hooked and see benefits, they will most likely apt for an extended version of the service and upgrade to the complete one. You're maintaining the quality of your brand while still offering an affordability factor no one is competing with.

This segues nicely into the process of adding value to existing services. Let's say your competitor is advertising a color and cut service for half price and all of your clients start running next door to get their colors done by them now. If you don't do something fast, you'll have to close your doors.

You panic and think, geez; maybe I should offer the same price. You know this is going to hurt your brand and your bottom line. Then, the strategist comes alive in you and you think, maybe instead I can offer something in addition to their full-priced service. So, instead of competing in price wars, you're in a whole new league.

Maybe when they get the color service you also toss in a color gloss and conditioning treatment as an added value. It's a tasty treat that many clients will consider and try. And once they do, they're hooked. Their hair has never looked or felt more luxurious. They realize you can't put a price on beauty. So you just saved a customer and added new revenue in future sales when the price wars have diminished. Your quality brand is alive and thriving, while your competitor's brand is destroyed because she'll never be able to raise her prices back to normal and have clients feeling half as good as yours do.

You're not discounting what you do best; you're simply adding a boatload of value to it.

CREATE SUSTAINABLE PASSION

So it's a few years from now, clients are flowing, phone lines are ringing, talented stylists are begging you for a place in your salon, and heck, let's throw in this great new equation that you've got the entire local news team of personalities as clients and they scroll the name of your salon in the final show credits. You've done it all. You've reached your dreams and beyond. Then you take a deep breath and ask yourself this question: *What now*?

Think this won't happen? It happens to the best of the best. Just look at the long list of celebrities who sabotage their careers because they, too, find themselves in that precarious position of accomplishing everything they set out to do and are now laden with boredom. Why does this happen? Because these people failed at one major component in life. They failed to attach meaning and value to their dreams so they are left feeling empty even though they've got more than enough to fill the void. They failed to find a deep meaning beyond just the money to sustain them over the long-term.

So, here we are again facing the same exact question I first asked you at the beginning of this book. Why are you going (or why did you go) into business for yourself? If your answer is because you just love what you do, because you crave to be surrounded by it all the time, because you want to do it the way you think it should be done, then congratulations. You've got real motivation that will carry you over any obstacle, through any brambles, and across any raging river threatening to drown you.

Do yourself a HUGE favor and write this sentence down and read it often: I have a passion for all things salon and beauty related, and this is why I am a small business success.

If you can tap into passionate emotions and really go for this endeavor because it's who you are and it's in your core, then you will go far and the money will follow. The money will work for you instead of you for it.

Success really comes down to setting goals that are personally rewarding and emotionally strong, to planning and thinking things through on a strategic level, to focusing and refocusing on tactics until they feel right, to measuring your actions and ensuring you're being as effective as you can, and mostly, it boils down to having a deep love and passion for being a part of something greater than yourself.

Now roll up your sleeves. You have some salon buzz to create!

Endnotes

(1) Chapter Two

Michael E. Gerber, *The E-Myth Revisited: Why Most Small Businesses Don't Work and What to Do About It* (New York: HarperCollins, 1995), 97.

(2) Chapter Three

Kerry Patterson, Joseph Grenny, Ron McMillan, Al Switler, *Crucial Conversations: Tools for Talking When Stakes are High* (New York: McGraw-Hill, 2002), 27.

(3) Chapter Five

Michael E. Gerber, *The E-Myth Revisited: Why Most Small Businesses Don't Work and What to Do About It* (New York: HarperCollins, 1995), 194.

Resources

- The US Small Business Association: www.sba.gov
- SCORE: www.score.org/explore_score.html
- Government information: www.business.gov
- Keywords and SEO information: Adwords.google.com
- Advertising opportunities: www.groupons.com | www.livingsocial.com
- Website consultants, templates, hosting packages: www.maximwebsites.com | www.godaddy.com
- HTML email templates: www.mailchimp.com
- Twitter applications: www.tweetdeck.com | www.hootsuite.com

Made in the USA
Middletown, DE
06 June 2016